WILDCATS!
OF NORTH AMERICA

BOBCAT

By Jalma Barrett
Photographs by Larry Allan

BLACKBIRCH PRESS, INC.
WOODBRIDGE, CONNECTICUT

Published by Blackbirch Press, Inc.
260 Amity Road
Woodbridge, CT 06525

e-mail: staff@blackbirch.com
Web site: www.blackbirch.com

Printed in the United States

10 9 8 7 6 5 4 3 2 1

Dedication
For Pamela

–JB and LA

Library of Congress Cataloging-in-Publication Data
Barrett, Jalma.
Bobcat / by Jalma Barrett : photographs by Larry Allan.
    p.   cm. — (Wildcats of North America)
   Includes bibliographical references (p. 24) and index.
   Summary: Describes the bobcat and its natural habitat, including physical traits, social life, survival instincts, birth and development, and interaction with humans.
   ISBN 1-56711-257-9 (lib. bdg. : alk. paper)
   1. Bobcat—Juvenile literature. [1. Bobcat.] I. Allan, Larry, ill. II. Title.
III. Series: Barrett, Jalma. Wildcats of North America.
QL737.C23B2653   1999
599.75'36—dc21
                                                      98-9878
                                                     CIP
                                                     AC

Contents

Introduction—A Cat Named "Bob"

If you were a large wild cat living somewhere in North America, your name would probably be "Bob." Bobcats are the most common species of wildcat found in North America—and they are found only on this continent. That includes Southern Canada, the United States (except in the prairies) and in parts of Mexico. Bobcats are most common in America's Far West—especially in California, Idaho, Utah, Nevada, Montana, Wyoming, Washington, and Oregon. Bobcats can even be found in New Jersey!

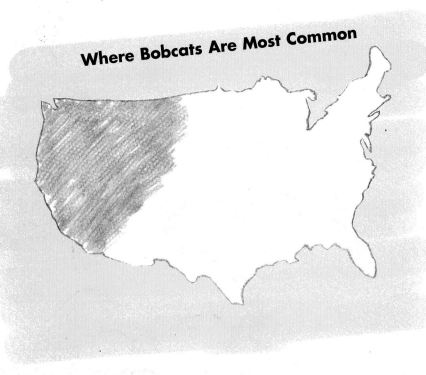

Where Bobcats Are Most Common

Bobcats live in canyons, forests, densely shrubby areas, and swamps. They stay wherever they can find plenty of food, and cover in which to hide. They prefer scrubby countryside or evergreen forests. They also like rocky or brushy dry areas, like the American Southwest.

Bobcats are North America's most common large wildcat.

The Bobcat Body

Bobcats have short (*bobbed*) tails about 6 inches (15 cm) long. That's where they actually get their name. The color of bobcats is *tawny* (yellow-brown or golden tan), but they become more gray in winter. These cats are spotted and they have stripes or bar markings in their coats. Their upper legs often have dark, or black, bars on them. Most bobcats weigh about 38 pounds (17 kilograms). That's more than three times the weight of an average house cat. Bobcats are 18 to 26 inches (45 to 66 cm) tall at the shoulder; which is about twice the shoulder height of an average house cat.

In some areas, bobcats have tufts (spikes of hair) on the ends of their ears.

Bobcats are usually golden-tan or gray.

A short, bobbed tail distinguishes the bobcat.

In other areas, bobcats only have very small ear tufts, which are hardly visible at all. Bobcats have extra long fur on each side of their faces. This fur is called *muttonchops*. They make bobcats look like they're wearing big bow ties! Their legs seem to be long in relation to their body size. Like your companion house cat, bobcats can swim, but they don't like to.

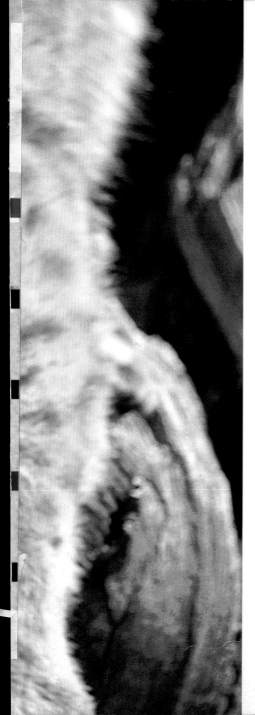

Special Features

Most wild cats actually have a poor sense of smell. They don't track their prey by smelling it. Instead, they rely on keen vision and excellent hearing to hunt. A cat's eyes collect light and reflect it back out. This gives cats excellent night vision. Have you ever seen a cat's eyes "shine" in the dark when they reflect a car's headlights? That's an example of the way this very special eye works.

The ears of a bobcat have less movement than do the ears of your favorite house cat—that is, their ears swivel less. A bobcat carries its ears erect and pointing forward. It will lay its ears back only when it is angry. In response to a sound, a bobcat will turn its head to look and to hear better. This gives it information from its two keenest senses at the same time.

A bobcat will lay its ears back when it is angry.

9

Social Life

Bobcats are usually only seen together at mating time. They prefer to live alone. Each cat's territory is well marked. Bobcats mark their territories with urine sprayed on trees or with feces (droppings). Sometimes they scrape the soil with their paws to cover their feces, which further marks each spot. All cats need scratching posts. Bobcats scratch on trees, which leaves their scent there as well. They also have anal scent glands under the base of the tail, which they use to leave scents and mark their territories.

Most bobcats prefer to live alone.

Certain trees in a bobcat's territory are marked by scratching.

These scents provide odor "information" about each territory's resident bobcat that other bobcats can recognize. Bobcat territories include tracks, dens, and resting places.

Bobcats are most active at night. After hunting and eating, they like to spend their days resting. Although they are expert climbers, they don't spend much time in trees. Occasionally, a bobcat will rest in the lower branches of a tree or on a big rock.

Expert Hunters

Bobcats hunt with patience and cleverness. They creep as close as possible—called *stalking*—staying low to the ground and hiding behind bushes and rocks. Then they make a sudden rush when they're close to the prey. If an animal runs, the bobcat will chase it. Their long reach and large paws allow them to pounce on the backs of their prey. Bobcats bite their victim's throat, base of the skull, or chest to bring it down.

Bobcats hunt as they travel around their territories. To be successful stalkers, bobcats have learned to move silently. While stalking, their excellent vision shows them where they can step silently with their forefeet. They always step with their hind paws where they've already stepped with their front paws. This way, the bobcat knows it can step without making any noise, which could warn their prey that a stalker is nearby.

Hiding behind bushes and rocks is part of hunting.

Inset and above: Stalking requires a bobcat to move slowly, stay close to the ground, and to get as close to prey as possible before pouncing.

Bobcats will rest in spaces between rocks, in a thicket, or in some other hiding place during the day. Sometimes they will hide beside a trail, waiting for a small meal to hop by. This kind of hunting is called an *ambush*. In winter, bobcats have been known to wait in one spot for so long that clumps of their fur get frozen in the snow. These places are called *hunting beds*.

The Food Supply

A bobcat sits in a hunting bed.

A bobcat's favorite food is the snowshoe hare (in the northern U.S.) or cottontail rabbit (in the eastern U.S.). A bobcat's *canine teeth* (four long, sharp pointed teeth) are spaced just far enough apart to separate the *vertebra* (bones in the spine) of its favorite prey. Bobcats eat other animals, too—even bats. They are fond of opossums, moles, shrews, raccoons, domestic cats, small deer, woodchucks, foxes, porcupines, skunks, birds, and reptiles.

Bobcats can *fast* (go without eating for a period of time) when food isn't readily available. They also will *cache* (hide) larger prey, such as a deer that has only been partially eaten. Then they'll return to the cache later. Smaller prey, such as rabbits, are usually eaten all at once. Bobcats eat a great deal when food is plentiful, just in case their food sources suddenly run out.

But they don't always catch what they stalk. In fact, they may stalk something 6 to 10 times before they actually catch their prey.

If food is very scarce, bobcats will eat dead animals they happen upon (*carrion*). These carrion are usually animals that have been killed by cars or by hunters.

The ability of the bobcat to exist on a wide variety of prey, as well as its willingness to live in a variety of habitats, have helped to make their populations strong and stable.

Eating a snowshoe hare.

The Mating Game

Bobcats over two years old mate in February or March. Female bobcats usually mate every two years. In some areas in the southern United States, they've been known to have two litters in a year. Protected places, such as caves, hollow logs, and rocky ledges, are used as extra dens or resting places by bobcats. A maternal den (for having babies) will have a nest of leaves and other dry vegetation, which other dens will not have. More than one male may want to mate with a female, but only the *dominant* (strongest) male will. The pair may mate several times after a courtship that includes a series of chases and ambushes. The female may also mate with other males.

Bobcats are usually only seen together during mating season.

Kittens

Two to four baby bobcats are born in late April or early May. This is usually 62 days after the parents mate. Litters may be as small as a single kitten, or they might include as many as 7. Kittens are born well furred and spotted, but they're quite helpless. At 1 month old, kittens begin to explore and play near their den. They're *weaned* (cut off from breastfeeding) when they reach 2 months of age. By autumn, at 5 or 6 months old, the kittens are already hunting on their own. Still, they remain with their mother for nearly a year.

Left: Bobcat kittens are furry and helpless.
Opposite: Kittens usually stop breastfeeding when they reach 2 months of age.

Male bobcats play no part in raising their kittens. The mothers do it all—clean, feed, protect, and teach their young until they're almost as big as she is.

Kittens are well protected by their mother, but they are still at risk. Some predators, like foxes, owls, and even adult male bobcats, may prey upon young bobcats.

By 4 to 6 weeks of age, kittens are exploring on their own.

A Tale of Two Tails

The bobcat and its close "cousin," the lynx, are often mistaken for each other because both have shortened tails. Actually, the tail of a lynx is usually 2 to 6 inches (5 to 15 cm) long. A bobcat's tail is usually between 4 and 7 inches (10 to 18 cm) long. It would be pretty hard to tell the difference in length, if you saw one. The bobcat's tail is colored differently, however. A bobcat tail is black on the top, but not on the underside. A lynx tail has a black tip—including black on the underside. The lynx can weigh over 80 pounds (36 kilograms) (about twice the weight of a bobcat), though many lynx can be more bobcat-sized. There are other differences, too. A lynx has long ear tufts, while a bobcat has short ear tufts. The bobcat is more brown in color, and has dark bars on its forelegs. Lynx are grayer and have longer fur than bobcats. The lynx has much larger feet and longer legs than a bobcat, too.

Bobcats make sounds that often sound like house cats. A bobcat's scream can be piercing. If a bobcat is threatened, it will make a sort of *cough-bark* sound from deep in its throat. It will also show its teeth in a threatening way. Like domestic cats, bobcats scream loudest and most frequently during the mating season. Bobcats also purr, just like the feline friends you may know.

In the wild, bobcats do not often reach 10 years of age. But they do live two or three times that long in *captivity* (in zoos).

Bobcats and Humans

Even though bobcats are protected by laws in most states, humankind is still a bobcat's worst enemy. People hunt them, sometimes for "fun" or in the name of "sport." Automobiles kill many bobcats, too. As much as some lawmakers try to protect animals like the bobcat, these laws are very difficult to enforce. People used to trap bobcats for their fur. Some shot bobcats as nuisances, especially farmers who thought the cats were attacking livestock. Actually, bobcats help farmers by feeding on animals who do destroy crops, like rabbits and mice.

Bobcats need to be left alone in order to survive.

A bobcat may look a lot like a large house cat, but it is a wild animal. You should avoid any contact with one, even though they are beautiful. People call bobcats wildcats. That should remind you to look, but do not try to touch—if you're lucky enough to come upon one. Bobcats are not like house cats. In fact, you should never try to touch any animal you don't know and who doesn't know you.

Because of its adaptability, the future is bright for the bobcat. "Bob" doesn't mind having humans nearby, as long as they leave him alone. In peace and quiet, the bobcat is free to remain what it is meant to be: a truly wild cat.

Feline Facts

Name: Bobcat

Scientific Name: *Felis lynx rufus*

Shoulder Height: 18" to 26" (45 to 66 cm)

Body Length: 24" to 42" (61 cm to 1.06 meter)

Tail Length: 4" to 7" (10 to 18 cm)

Weight: approx. 38 pounds (17 kilograms)

Color: Tawny (golden tan)

Reaches sexual maturity at: 2 years

Females mate: Once every 2 years

Gestation (pregnancy period): 62 days

Litter Size: 1 to 7 kittens (usual size is 2 to 4)

Social Life: Lives alone

Favorite Food: Hare or rabbit

Habitat: Varied. Widespread in U.S. Also southern Canada, northern Mexico

Glossary

ambush To hide and then attack.

cache A hidden supply.

canine teeth The four pointed teeth on each side of the upper and lower jaws.

captivity Not wild or free; taken out of the wild and not able to leave an enclosed area.

carrion Dead prey that was not hunted.

dominant Most powerful.

fast To go without food for a long period of time.

feces Bodily wastes; droppings.

muttonchops Side whiskers.

stalking To hunt or track in a quiet, secret way; usually following prey.

vertebra One of the small bones that make up the backbone.

Further Reading

Arnold, Caroline A. *Bobcats* (Early Bird Nature Books). Minneapolis, MN: Lerner Publications Company, 1997.

Arnold, Caroline A. *Cats: In from the Wild.* Minneapolis, MN: Carolrhoda Books, 1993.

Hodge, Deborah. *Wild Cats: Cougars, Bobcats and Lynx.* Ontario: Kids Can Press, 1997.

Ryden, Hope. *Your Cat's Wild Cousins.* New York: Lodestar Books, 1992.

Index